THIS CANDLEWICK BOOK BELONGS TO:

_____

_____

_____

First U.S. paperback edition 2009

Library of Congress Cataloging-in-Publication Data is available.

Library of Congress Catalog Card Number 2007052204

ISBN 978-0-7636-4029-3 (hardcover)
ISBN 978-0-7636-4512-0 (paperback)

WKT 22
16

Printed in Shenzhen, Guangdong, China

This book was typeset in ITCKabel.
The illustrations were created digitally.

Candlewick Press
99 Dover Street
Somerville, Massachusetts 02144

visit us at www.candlewick.com

CANDLEWICK PRESS

For
Charlotte
and Lauren

The author and publisher would like to thank Sue Ellis
at the Centre for Literacy in Primary Education, Martin Jenkins,
and Paul Harrison for their invaluable input and guidance
during the making of this book.

OSCAR and the CRICKET

A BOOK ABOUT MOVING AND ROLLING

Geoff Waring

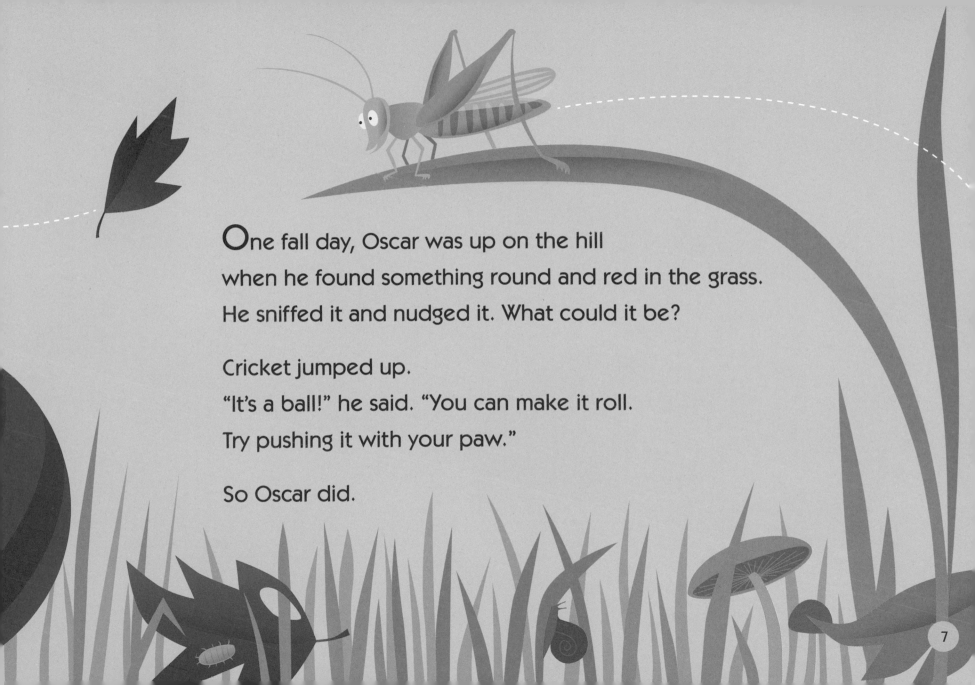

One fall day, Oscar was up on the hill
when he found something round and red in the grass.
He sniffed it and nudged it. What could it be?

Cricket jumped up.
"It's a ball!" he said. "You can make it roll.
Try pushing it with your paw."

So Oscar did.

The ball rolled away through the grass . . .

8

then lay still.

"Why did it stop?" Oscar asked.

"The thick grass slowed it down," Cricket said.

"Try rolling it on the path."

But a long branch was lying in the way.
"We'll have to move it," Cricket said.
"I'm not big or strong enough,
but you are, Oscar. Try giving it a pull."

"Uuuuurgh," Oscar groaned.
Slowly the branch started to move.

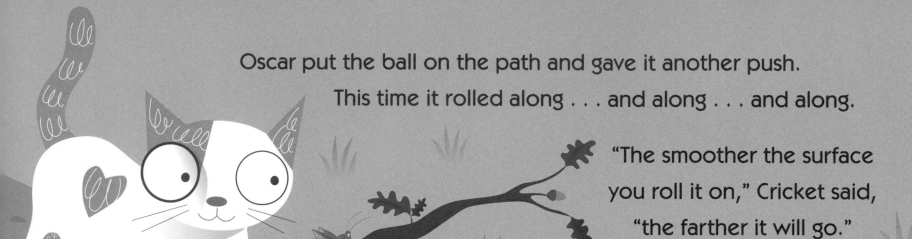

Oscar put the ball on the path and gave it another push.
This time it rolled along . . . and along . . . and along.

"The smoother the surface
you roll it on," Cricket said,
"the farther it will go."

"It's rolling in a straight line," Oscar noticed,

"and it's heading toward . . .

the tree!"

"Oh, dear!" Oscar said.
"It's all right," said Cricket.
"The ball hit the side
of the tree, and that made it
roll in a different direction."

BOUNCE!

For a moment, Oscar stopped watching the ball to look up. All the leaves were swaying and fluttering.

"The leaves can move
by themselves!" Oscar said.
"It looks like it," Cricket said,
"but the wind is pushing them
and making them move."

"Does everything need a push to make it move?" Oscar asked. "What about me?"

"You can move by yourself," Cricket said. "Most animals can. Our bodies have muscles to help us."

And he jumped UP . . .

... and **down.**

"Moving makes you change shape!" Oscar said, laughing.

"We can use our muscles to move ourselves and to move other things too," Cricket said.

A leaf-cutter ant can lift fifty times its own body weight in its jaws.

A hawfinch can crack a hard cherry pit in its bill.

A spider monkey can swing its whole body by its tail.

An elephant can pull down a tree branch with its trunk.

A dung beetle can push a ball of dung the size of an apple with its back legs.

Just then Oscar saw the ball again, lying in the grass. This time he gave it a great BIG push.

and it rolled through some leaves.

It rolled through some mud,

"Is it slowing down?" Oscar asked.

"Yes," Cricket said. "But it hasn't stopped.

You gave it such a strong push."

"Maybe it will never stop!"
Oscar said.

But just then,
a kitten put out a paw,
and the ball stopped.

"Hello," said Oscar. "I'm Oscar,
and this is Cricket. Who are you?"

"I'm Ted," said Ted.
"Can I play?"

Ted gave the ball a push.
Oscar ran after it.
"Look out!" called Cricket.

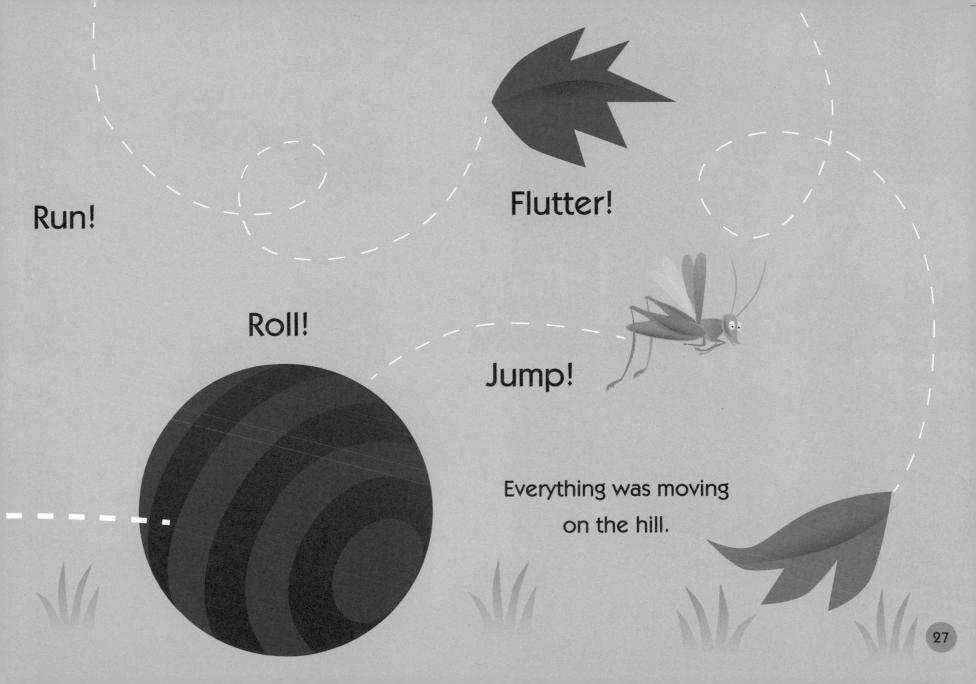

Run!

Flutter!

Roll!

Jump!

Everything was moving
on the hill.

Thinking about moving and rolling

On the hill, Oscar found out about these things:

Getting going

An object needs an outside force—a push or a pull—to start it moving.

A push

A pull

A push

Try moving different objects. Which ones can you push? Which ones can you pull? Are there some you can push *and* pull?

Keeping going

Once an object is moving, it travels in a straight line, unless something gets in the way.

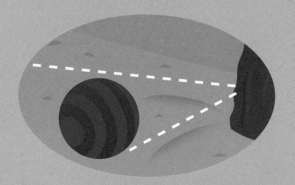

Bounce

See if you can make something move in two directions—try up and down or forward and backward.

Stopping

An object needs an outside force to make it stop moving, too.

The stronger the force, the more quickly it stops.

Stopping after a
short time

Stopping instantly

Stopping after a
long time

Try pushing a ball on a smooth surface and on a bumpy surface.

What do you notice?

Index

Look up the pages
to find out about these
"moving and rolling" things:

Oscar thinks moving and rolling are great! Do you think so, too?

Geoff Waring studied graphics in college and worked as an art director at *Elle*, *Red*, and *Vogue Australia* and as design director of *British Vogue*. He is currently creative director of *Glamour* magazine. He is the author and illustrator of the Oscar books, as well as the illustrator of *Black Meets White* by Justine Fontes. He says that the Oscar books are based on his own cat, Oskar. Geoff Waring lives in London.